TO AFROPHILES

BETTY & BRIA

WITH BEST WISHES

FROM

LET'S VISIT NAMIBIA

Special events

Wimpole Home Farm has many events, like lambing weekends, children's days and Meet Father Christmas. You can even have your birthday party here – just don't share your cake with the chickens! Visit our web site or give us a call.

By the way...

- Pushchairs and back-carriers welcome, and there is a children's play area.
- Book one of our 3 wheelchairs and bear in mind that there are some gravel areas.

Woolsthorpe Manor

Historic house   Discovery centre

23 Newton Way, Woolsthorpe-
by-Colsterworth, nr Grantham,
Lincolnshire, NG33 5NR
01476 860338

OPENING TIMES
House
4 Mar–26 Mar 1pm–5pm
Sat, Sun
29 Mar–1 Oct 1pm–5pm
Wed–Sun
7 Oct–29 Oct 1pm–5pm
Sat, Sun
Note
Open BHols and Good Fri:
1pm–5pm

ADMISSION PRICES
£4.50, child £2.20, family
£11.20, family (one adult) £6.70

The birthplace and family home of Sir Isaac Newton, the chap who discovered gravity when an apple fell on his head in this very garden. The apple tree's no more, though one of its descendants lives on. It's amazing to think that Newton had some of his most important and famous ideas in this modest little house.

Irritating Isaac
Newton may have been a clever-clogs but he was also known to be a bit cross and cantankerous. He was prone to disagree with royal astronomers, and had an argument with famous mathematician Leibniz that lasted over 15 years. Well, nobody said a genius has to be nice.

What to see
- A big display telling the story of the discovery of gravity. That's heavy!
- An edition of Newton's famous work *Principia,* first published in 1687. That's quite heavy too.
- All kinds of Newtonian gadgets in the shop.

What to do
- Wander around the orchards and paddocks.
- Visit the farm buildings with rare breed Lincoln Longwool sheep.
- Dip into the Science Discovery Centre, with a chance to look through telescopes, play with pendulums and more.

Special events
We have an apple day (well, we would….) and have had family learning days that take you back to the 17th century. Get in touch to see what's coming up.

By the way…
- There's a family guide and quiz/trail for you to have a go at. And pick up a leaflet to do a village walk.
- Baby-changing facilities, but bear in mind the café is small and has a limited selection (it's only open at weekends, too).
- You can book a wheelchair, though there are stairs to the upper floors.

Let's visit
NAMIBIA

D E GOULD

ACKNOWLEDGEMENTS

The Author and Publishers are grateful to the following organizations for permission to reproduce copyright material in this book:

Sigi Gross; Hutchison Photo Library; The Mansell Collection; Nature Photographers Ltd; Oxfam; Rossing Uranium Ltd; Photos, State Archives Windhoek.

First published 1988

Published by
MACMILLAN PUBLISHERS LTD
Houndmills, Basingstoke, Hampshire RG21 2XS
and London
Companies and representatives
throughout the world

Designed and produced by Burke Publishing Company Limited
Pegasus House, 116-120 Golden Lane
London EC1Y 0TL, England.

Printed in Hong Kong

British Library Cataloguing in Publication Data
Gould, Dennis.
    Let's visit Namibia.—(Let's visit).
    1.   Namibia—Social life and customs
    —Juvenile literature
    I.   Title
    968.8'03   DT703
    ISBN 0-333-45523-1

Contents

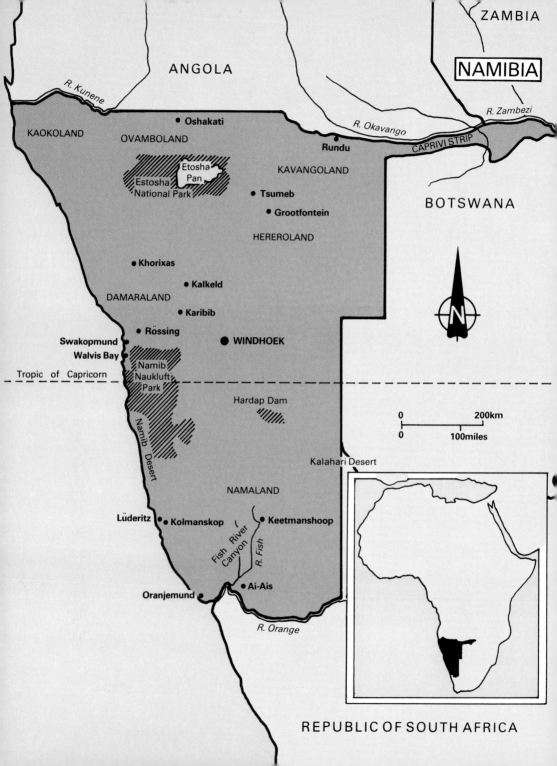

The Land between Two Deserts

Namibia is a country which has been very much in the news in recent decades. The country's struggle for independence has been drawn-out and bitterly contested. The Namibians have sought to free themselves from domination by the neighbouring state of South Africa, first by negotiations and then by guerilla warfare. Their case has been supported by the United Nations Organization and by most countries of the world. However, South Africa has been slow to give up its control of the country and has been accused of "dragging its feet".

But struggling has long been a way of life for the people of this land. Over the centuries, Namibia has seen many struggles for political control of the territory, both by the indigenous population against various colonizing nations, and between the numerous tribes which make up that indigenous population.

Even more than political struggle, life in Namibia has been a struggle against the harsh environment. Periodic prolonged droughts are an accepted fact of life for people who live in a country where desert and semi-desert conditions prevail. Namibia has been called "The Land between Two Deserts".

It is a large country, but it is one of the least densely populated countries in the world. With an area of more than 800,000 square kilometres (over 300,000 square miles), it is nearly four

The dried-up Swakop River. Namibia faces a continual struggle against drought

times the size of the United Kingdom and larger than the US state of Texas. On average, there is about one square kilometre of land to every inhabitant (roughly five people to every two square miles).

Before the country was officially recognized by the name of Namibia, it was called South West Africa, and this clearly indicates where it is situated. Along the 1,400-kilometre (900-mile) Atlantic coastline of the country lies the Namib Desert, with enormous sand-dunes bearing hardly any vegetation. It is said to be the oldest desert in the world. This is a strip of inhospitable and almost uninhabited sandy desert, some eighty to 120 kilometres (fifty to seventy-five miles) in width. It occupies one-fifth of the surface area of Namibia and is famous for the towering sand-dunes of the Soussuvlei which, at about

8

350 metres (over one thousand feet), are considered to be amongst the highest in the world. This arid desert is a strange sight so close to the vast ocean.

The land rises in terraces towards the east. The high plateaux are between 1,000 and 2,000 metres (3,000 and 6,000 feet) above sea level. The central plateau of the territory comprises more than half the area of Namibia. This landscape offers startling contrasts, ranging from rugged mountains and rocky outcrops to sand-filled valleys and endless vistas of plains. The highest mountains are the Brandberg (2585 metres—about 8,000 feet) and the Moltkeblick, which is just slightly lower.

The grasslands and bush of the highlands gradually become more sparse and, on the eastern side of the country, once again become desert. This is the Kalahari Desert, known in the local language as *Kalakgadi* ("The Thirst Lands"). The Kalahari extends far into neighbouring Botswana, from which country Namibia is separated by a man-made border. The Kalahari Desert is less fiercely arid than the Namib Desert, and its reddish sands nourish a surprising variety of drought-resistant plants, which in turn provide food for birds and animals. There are even some prosperous sheep and cattle-farms in the area.

In the south and north, the country's borders are formed by the only two permanently-flowing rivers in Namibia. North of the Kunene River lies the neighbouring country of Angola. In the south, the Orange River forms the border with the Cape Province of the Republic of South Africa.

In the extreme north-east, a long narrow strip of land between

The towering sand dunes of the Sossusvlei

Botswana and Zambia stretches for some 500 kilometres
(300 miles), from the Okarango River at the western end to
the Zambezi in the east. This region is known as the Caprivi
Strip.

Namibia also has a common border point with Zimbabwe.
This is a very unusual situation, as the borders of four countries
meet at a point in the middle of the Zambezi River. They are
Zambia, Zimbabwe, Botswana and Namibia.

Although much of the country is in the Tropics, the climate is
typical of a semi-desert land. The days are hot and the nights are
cool. In the height of summer, in the months of December and
January, the shade temperatures reach more than 40 degrees
Celsius (around 100 degrees Fahrenheit) but there is often little
shade to be found. During the winter months, six months later,

10

the days are pleasantly warm but the temperature may fall to a few degrees below freezing-point at dawn.

There are two sources of relief from the high temperatures: along the coast, the cold Benguella Current has a cooling effect; up on the high central plateau, it is less hot than in the other inland areas. The Benguella Current causes dense fogs in all seasons other than summer. These usually build up in the late afternoon and do not clear before the next mid-morning. These moisture-laden mists play a very important part in the ecology of the Namib Desert, as they bring water to an otherwise dry and arid region, enabling some plants and animals to survive.

For much of the year there are dry and cloudless conditions throughout the country. The sun shines, on average, for more

Fishing on the Okavango River

than three hundred days of the year. Rainfall is usually fairly regular and comes during two periods. A minor rainfall usually occurs at some time during the last three months of the year, and the main rains are awaited eagerly by man, beast and plant, in heavy, concentrated downpours between mid-January and April. They are usually accompanied by quite frequent, and often violent, thunderstorms. The average annual rainfall for the whole country hardly reaches 100 millimetres (about four inches) but this varies considerably from region to region. Unfortunately, what little rainfall there is, is not particularly effective because much of it evaporates in the heat, or trickles away before it can soak into the ground.

More rain falls in the northern areas, where it averages about 400 millimetres (sixteen inches) per annum. In the Kavango and Eastern Caprivi districts the average is twice as high.

Although this picture of a land with a sparse population, living in a largely inhospitable landscape under blazing sun, may not sound very aluring, Namibia is in fact a most fascinating country.

Visitors are struck by the variety of beautiful birds and animals, and intrigued by the way in which many have adapted to the difficult conditions. The plant-life, too, offers examples which are unique to this part of the world.

To the south stretch the endless plains with spectacular wonders of nature, and farms where "Persian lamb" fleeces are obtained from karakul sheep. To the west is the Namib Desert where some of the most rare reptiles in the world are found, and where a gracefully attractive antelope—the oryx—survives

12

An ox-drawn sand sled in the Okavango district of Caprivi

almost incredibly amongst the arid dunes. Here, too, grows the remarkable welwitschia, a tree which lives for hundreds of years. To the east is the Kalahari Desert, with the characteristic camel-thorn trees and wide-ranging cattle ranches.

Namibia is still a young country from the point of view of development. At the same time it is ancient, with dinosaur tracks from primaeval times still to be seen imprinted in rock formations.

The description "a harsh paradise" aptly suits Namibia. With allusion to its riches in diamonds, it also claims the title "Africa's Gem".

The People

Although Namibia is a large country, it has comparatively few inhabitants and they are very varied in race, origin, appearance and language. Most of these different groups arrived in Namibia only in the course of the last four hundred years.

Current statistics give the total population as around one million, although conditions in the country make it difficult to obtain a reliable census figure. Some people think that the real population figure may be as high as one and a half million.

It is generally agreed, however, that by far the largest ethnic group is the Ovambo, who make up nearly half the total population. The Ovambo are divided into some seven or eight different tribes. Each tribe has its own territory and speaks a dialect of one of two languages.

The majority of Namibia's population live on the high plateau and more than half inhabit the northern third of the land. It is here that the Ovambo are concentrated.

The traditional lifestyle of the Ovambo is dependent on the flood waters which come down to Ovamboland after the annual rains in Angola. These flood-waters are called *efundja*. In good years they provide the inhabitants with enough water for them to be able to maintain their traditional way of life. The flood-waters also carry with them fish which are caught and eaten.

14

Two young Namibians

Surplus fish are smoked or dried, to be stored for future use.

The people live in a cluster of homesteads which may give the appearance of having been built in a very haphazard manner with an irregular pattern of passageways and fences. But they are, in fact, well planned. Originally they were built in this way in order to make it easy to defend the home and *kraal* and protect it from attack. (The word *kraal* is used in Southern Africa to refer to an area within a fence; this may be an individual home, or even a village or, very often, an enclosure for cattle only).

15

Nowadays, the structure is based more on tradition than necessity.

The *kraal* of the headman is often surrounded by a high fence which may be as much as 200 metres (220 yards) in length. The tree trunks and branches of which it is built may be as high as three metres (ten feet). These form a strong palisade. The other enclosures are smaller, but they are still arranged to provide security for three, or more, separate huts. A thorn-bush fence, which is virtually impenetrable, serves to keep the cattle and goats enclosed; at the same time it protects them from wild animals.

The day-to-day work is very clearly divided between the male and female members of the society. A young boy soon learns about his father's role and all about the cattle which he will have to tend. Cattle are regarded as a status symbol and they are seldom slaughtered for food, other than for special occasions, accompanied by ritual and celebrations. The Ovambo obtain their supply of meat from smaller animals, especially goats and chickens; even dogs may form part of the diet. A young boy also learns from the adult men how to build the protection around the home, as well as the skills of hunting.

The women look after the household. Their duties include fetching and carrying water, and working on the land. They grow sorghum, millet, beans, pumpkins, groundnuts and yams (sweet potatoes). They winnow the grain and grind it into flour. The men help out with heavier manual work, but it is the task of the womenfolk to build the hut.

As in many other parts of Africa, deforestation (clearing an area of trees) is a major problem. Much of the woodland has been destroyed as a result of people collecting wood for building and fuel, leaving a bare, tree-less plain. The only trees which the Ovambo not not cut down are the wild fruit trees which produce the plum-like marula, as well as figs and nuts.

The local type of palm-tree provides the people with many of their requirements. It is the source of a sweet, intoxicating drink, as well as food, and of material for plaiting into baskets and mats. This large palm produces fruit which are enjoyed by baboons and elephants. The hard white kernels resemble ivory, and are used to make ornaments, trinkets and curios.

A feature of traditional Ovambo culture is that the family name and wealth are passed down from one generation to the next on the mother's side of the family. This is called matrilineal descent. A maternal uncle (that is, the brother of the children's mother) has a more important role than their father. This system leads to certain complications and disadvantages and is slowly changing, perhaps all the more rapidly with Western influence. Nowadays, the male is more dominant in Ovambo society.

Western influence has also resulted in many Ovambo abandoning their traditional lifestyle and family, and seeking new means of making a living and gaining status. This influence previously made itself felt through Christianity, and included the alteration of the accepted tradition of a man having more than one wife. However, the Ovambo are the largest single

A Himba woman and her child

ethnic group in Namibia, and many of them still follow the centuries-old pattern of life, regulated by the seasonal *efundja.*

Also living in the north are the Kaokolanders, one of the smaller ethnic groups, the Kavangos, and the Himba. There are nearly seventy thousand Kavangos of five different tribes, and they speak three different languages. Being isolated in this area of the land, the Herero-speaking Himba people and their

18

neighbours, the Kaokolanders, have changed their traditional lifestyle very little.

Arid hills and craggy mountain ranges form the main part of Kaokoland, until the region merges into the bleak desert of the northern Kalahari. In the dry season, the terrain is rugged and sun-scorched; but it is rapidly changed by fierce rains from dusty, flat land into swampy, low-lying ground. Then the dry, sandy river-beds are filled with flooding torrents.

It is in these difficult conditions that the Himba people tend their cattle. The whole existence of the Himba revolves around cattle, which are a symbol of wealth and status. The Himba's main source of food is the milk provided by the cattle; it is often curdled by adding various herbs. Meat is reserved for special occasions. The skins of the animals provide clothing and footwear, as well as many other articles such as pouches, bags and ground-sheets. Himba men also use their cattle as a form of money to pay for a bride.

The herdsman has to learn to protect his cattle. Although he may be equipped with bow and arrow, club or spear, he relies a great deal on putting down herbal poisons which he knows to be effective, even against large predatory animals. Alternatively, he uses traps to protect his herd from predators.

In order to stress the importance of cattle in the lives of the Himba, a number of the animals are treated in special ways and are regarded as "sacred". For example, a father cuts pieces from the ears of specially selected heifers for his eldest son to wear. These are presented at name-giving ceremonies and at other important rites, such as initiation ceremonies, throughout the young boy's life.

Similarly, the extreme importance of keeping a fire alive and readily available has given the fire-stick a "sacred" value. In every family there is strict training to ensure that the eldest son is worthy of taking over the fire-stick from his father, to indicate that he is the new family leader.

It is possible to tell the social position of individual Himba simply by looking at their hair-style. The older men wear leather twisted around their heads, and their hair is not cut. But the younger men have shaven heads, except for a central strip which is woven into a single plait hanging down over their shoulders. To show that a woman is married, she lengthens her own hair with hair cut from the head of her brother. This is surmounted by a special marriage head-dress (called *erembe*) which is made of leather. Both men and women adorn themselves with beads, bangles and brooches. The women apply a cosmetic made from myrrh—a gum resin used in perfumes.

The Himba are part of a larger group of Herero-speakers. The original Herero probably came to Namibia from the north-east some four centuries ago. Some settled in the north of the country, along the Okavango River, and are now called the Mbanderu. Others settled in the Kaokoveld—the wild grass-lands of Kaokoland. However, after struggles with the Ovambo tribe for access to more fertile areas, many moved on, leaving the Himba behind.

There are subdivisions amongst the Herero-speaking peoples. One such group are the Tjimba, who gave up their pastoral way of life and became hunters and food-gatherers. Then there are the Thwa—traditionally the ironsmiths who provide the Himba with their throwing spears and many other items. Two other tribes—the Zemba and Hakaona—are closely related to the Herero and have, for centuries, provided the medicine-men and the water-diviners.

The social order of the Herero is both complicated and unusual. It is based on a system of double descent which is exclusive to the Herero people of Namibia. Each person belongs to two families, or social groupings: the *oruzo* of the father and the *eanda* of the mother.

In southern Africa, the name Herero most often conjures up a mental picture of the stately bearing of the women of this group. They are easily and immediately recognized by their unusual and colourful dress and headwear. A hundred years or more ago, European missionaries went to great lengths to encourage the African tribes to cover their near-naked bodies; the Herero women did so by copying the style of dress worn by the missionaries' wives, and they have worn the same style ever since. They made their dresses from odd scraps of brighly-coloured cloth, which they skilfully combined in a distinctive patchwork pattern. This dress is topped by a high and wide headpiece stiffened at the top to create a wing-like appearance.

The original inhabitants of Namibia, who are commonly referred to as Bushmen, live in the desert regions—in the north-east of the Namib and in the Kalahari.

Herero women in their colourful traditional dress at an outdoor health education class

There are now probably less than fifteen thousand Bushmen, and their lifestyle as hunters and people who can survive on the food they find growing wild in the veld is rapidly changing. Their primitive, remote existence is being encroached upon by advancing "civilization", so that probably only a couple of thousand are still living as their ancestors did for centuries.

The Dzu/wa Bushmen (the / indicates one of the clicking sounds that are a feature of the Bushman languages) are the only Bushmen still living in Namibia as hunters and food-gatherers. The Dzu/wa are part of the larger group of Bushmen known as !Kung. (The ! indicates a different type of clicking sound from /.)

These nomadic Bushmen wander in small bands of some

fifteen to twenty people. They wear little clothing and that is made mainly from animal skins. They have, after generations of living in the desert and semi-desert, learnt to survive where "civilized" man would not last for many days. For food, and even more importantly for liquid intake, they know which plants are edible or hold supplies of precious water. Often these lie hidden beneath the sandy surface and are probed out by the use of digging-sticks. Sometimes the moisture is sucked up from under ground by means of a kind of elongated drinking-straw, put together with lengths of hollow grass or plant stems. This life-saving water may be stored in gourds or in the large eggshells of the ostrich. The Bushmen carry the gourds or shells with them or bury them in hiding-places from which they may be collected in the future.

Some plants are more easily available and they form the basis of the Bushman's diet. Altogether, about one hundred plants are known to him as being edible. Meat is of lesser importance and so hunting (by the men) plays a smaller part in the daily routine than the gathering of plants, insects and small animals (by the women). They may walk great distances in search of food. The men gather honey from the honeycombs of wild bees, often being guided to this hidden food by the honeybird.

Hunting is done by the use of poisonous arrows, fired from carefully constructed bows. The tip of the arrow is smeared with a lethal substance which is obtained from the chrysalis of certain beetles. The Bushman has to be extremely careful how he prepares and handles this deadly poison.

The hunt may be a long process and often includes clever imitation of the prey to lure the animal into the open. The poisonous arrow does not kill the prey immediately and the hunters often have to track the wounded creature for long distances, before it finally collapses and dies, or they catch up and kill it.

The Bushmen live in a temporary camp, protected by simple shelters constructed from the few available branches and leaves.

Bushmen are, perhaps, best known for their rock-paintings. Hundreds of these paintings are still to be found in caves or on more protected rock faces. Most of them depict hunting scenes, usually with well-drawn animals—though the human figures tend to be more symbolic, rather like matchstick-men. There is a magnificent collection of more than three thousand

Bushman hunters

Bushman rock paintings at Twyfelfontein

rock paintings at Twyfelfontein, in the north-west of Namibia.

There are also Bushman engravings. Their origins and age are still a mystery. It is thought that the engravings may have been done by ancient hunters who lived thousands of years ago in the Early Stone Age, whereas the paintings are the work of Bushmen who came to the area much later.

Unfortunately, it seems there are no longer any Bushmen who carry on the original traditional art form. But they still express themselves readily in dance. Happiness and grief both find expression in dance, and it is also performed just as entertainment. In addition, the dance may have religious significance and sometimes culminates in a state of trance. The Bushmen combine their graceful movement and beautiful singing into a remarkable pattern of natural rhythm.

In certain fairly limited areas, further south, live the Damaras. There are about seventy-five thousand of these dark-skinned people of unknown origin. They differ completely from the other indigenous inhabitants. Their language is Nama.

Also living in these areas are the Nama people. They have light complexions, with yellow or reddish-brown skin, and are short in stature. The Nama who live in Namibia are part of the Khoikhoi group of people.

The Khoikhoi are like the Bushmen in appearance, with high cheek-bones and tapering chins. The fold of their upper eyelids gives their almond-shaped eyes the look of Mongolians. Also similar to the Bushmen are the click sounds in their speech.

It was these sounds which earned them the name of Hottentots. This name has become somewhat derogatory and is now in much less common usage, but originally it was derived from the Dutch word for a stammerer.

But the Khoikhoi are quite a separate group from the Bushmen, whom they call "San". The name "Khoisan" is used for both groups together.

One feature of the life of the Namibian Khoikhoi is the harvesting of the !Nara melon. These melons contain a sweet tasty pulp with a strong, distinctive smell. The pulp is boiled and the seeds removed to leave a clear purée which is poured out onto a clean area of sand. It is left for a couple of days before being turned, rather like a pancake. When the oil has been drained away from both sides and it is dry, it is cut into strips to form a delicacy, which is sucked or licked with great relish, thus

26

!Nara melons growing in the desert

removing any of the grains of sand still sticking to it. The seeds are not wasted but are dried in the sun; many are exported. In their dried form they are eaten like nuts.

One of the few trees which can survive in these arid regions is the acacia. Traditionally, the Nama used its bark to construct their homes. Now, more modern materials are used, but the resulting shacks are certainly not more attractive. The bark of the acacia can also provide food for the herds of goats and other animals, and even for the people themselves in times of extreme hunger.

Another small group in Namibia are the Rehoboth, who call themselves Basters. The Rehoboth Basters are a unique and mixed group, being descendants of wandering Europeans and

27

Nama. At the end of the eighteenth century, their ancestors were nomads.

There are also some few thousand Tswana, who are related to the inhabitants of neighbouring Botswana and of some parts of South Africa, especially Bophutatswana. In addition, some forty thousand East Caprivians live in the Caprivi Strip area, which has its own characteristic flora and fauna as a result of the much richer supplies of water.

The White population is concentrated in the central and southern part of the high plateau, especially around the capital, Windhoek. There are about one hundred thousand Whites. Some sixty-five per cent are Afrikaners (the descendants of

A township outside Windhoek

European settlers in South Africa, mainly of Dutch descent). About twenty-five per cent are of German origin, and approximately ten per cent have English ancestors.

The rest of the population is made up of about fifty thousand so-called Coloureds—people of mixed race. The Coloured community live mainly in the large towns, such as Windhoek, Keetmanshoop and Lüderitz.

With such a mixture of races it is, perhaps, not surprising that many of the people are able to converse in three, or even more, languages. The official languages of Namibia are Afrikaans (which has its origins in Dutch) and English. All official documents, notices and directional signs are in both languages. However, much German is still spoken, as a reminder of the years of German colonization. The most common African languages are Ovambo, Kavango and Herero. Besides these there are Nama and the Bushman languages, with their many fascinating click sounds. A written language called !Kung was developed for use in school instruction for Bushmen in the 1960s. Spelling rules were also devised but there were too many problems to overcome and the development ceased.

It is against this background of a wide variety of ethnic groups, with their differing cultures and languages, that present-day Namibia is trying to resolve its problems and ensure its independent future.

The Early History of Namibia

The earliest inhabitants of Namibia lived in the central and southern regions. They were the Bushmen, the Damara (sometimes called the Bergdama, or Mountain Dama) and the Nama.

The Bushmen have never cultivated land or reared herds of cattle. Instead, they have always been nomadic, moving continuously to new hunting-grounds. This is partly due to the fact that they have been constantly hounded by more powerful and aggressive tribes.

The Nama, too, are nomads; but, unlike the Bushmen, they have herds of cattle, fat-tailed sheep and goats.

Mystery still surrounds the origins of the Damara people. Although they share a common language with the Nama, which is unlike any other language in southern Africa, the two peoples are otherwise very different. The Damara have a much darker complexion than the Nama, who have yellow or reddish-brown skin. But the Damara, too, have always been nomadic hunters, living off the land.

By the beginning of the nineteenth century, the Nama tribes were waging fierce war with the groups living to the north of them—in particular, the Damara and Bushmen. These battles continued throughout the century.

The Herero, who had inhabited Kaokoland for many years and had adapted to this rugged region, began to migrate southwards in the early 1800s. (Some Herero-speaking groups, such as the Himba and Tjimba, remained in Kaokoland and live there to this day.)

The southward migration of the Herero led inevitably to fighting with the Nama people as they struggled for the same land on which to graze their cattle. Initially, the Herero were in a dominant position but, when the Nama received help from other Hottentot groups, the tide of events turned. These Hottentots had returned from Cape Province, in South Africa, where they had come into contact with guns and horses for the first time. The Herero were defeated in many bloody battles and were conquered by the Nama. But by 1860 the Herero, too, had obtained guns and had learnt how to use them. They rose against the Nama and, from then on, they seem to have been more often the victorious side in the inter-tribal skirmishes.

The Basters crossed the southern border, the Orange River, in 1868. The region was a battleground for the struggles between the Herero and the Nama, but the Basters succeeded, for the most part, in remaining neutral. They did, however, lose many cattle in raids by both the Bushmen and the Damara. In 1881, the Basters joined sides with the Nama tribes and the Afrikaners—the European settlers in South Africa, mainly of Dutch descent. And they launched a massive attack on the Herero.

During these years of more or less continuous tribal warfare,

31

the area was not colonized by European powers. As early as 1487, the Portuguese explorer Vasco da Gama had come to the conclusion that the Benguella Coast of southern Africa was of no value, and that the barren interior was even less worthy of interest.

Around the middle of the nineteenth century, however, a small number of settlers and explorers came up from the Cape of Good Hope. They were later followed by traders and missionaries. The first missionaries happened to be Germans, although they were actually operating through the London Missionary Society. They settled in an area called Transgariep, across the Gariep River—now called the Orange River.

The good intentions of the missionaries were all to often offset by the influence of the traders who exchanged liquor and guns for cattle.

The frequent battles between the different tribes in South West Africa led both the European settlers and the indigenous people themselves to request European powers, particularly Britain, to take over the area. They felt that this would give them some protection and provide stability in the territory. Britain, however, did not wish to extend its sovereignty beyond the port of Walvis Bay, which was taken over in 1878.

In 1880, a German trader named Lüderitz purchased from the Nama chiefs some land along the coast. This included Angra Pequena which he re-named Lüderitz. He paid £500 and sixty rifles for a 32-kilometre (20-mile) wide strip of coastal land which extended south from the Orange River for a distance of

Namatuni fort, built by the Germans in 1907. The fort stands in the vast Etosha National Park

some 400 kilometres (250 miles). Four years later, he arranged for this land to be placed under the protection of the German Empire. Bismarck, the German Chancellor at that time, was urged to extend German influence abroad, in line with other colonizing European powers.

Gradually, German authority over the area was extended, until it spread over the entire territory. In 1885, a treaty was signed between the Herero and Germany. All this took place without any opposition from Britain or any other of the European nations. Britain recognized German sovereignty over almost all of Namibia, including Caprivi. But Britain still controlled the only harbour along the coast, at Walvis Bay, which gave her command over trade in the area.

Between 1890 and 1894, German troops repeatedly attacked

33

the Nama, with little success. Germany wanted to set up a White settlement in the interior and the Germans in South West Africa continually played off one African group against another.

The tribal wars continued, even under German authority, although in 1898 there was a short period of peace in the south of the country. When, five years later, the Germans were busily engaged in quelling an uprising by a Nama tribe, the Herero took the opportunity to rebel in the central parts of the country. More than one hundred German men were killed there, their homes were burnt down and their cattle stolen. Forces were immediately sent from Germany to put down this uprising and a bloody battle ensued.

This battle between the Herero and the German forces lasted for several months and was extended by the fact that the Nama joined forces with the Herero.

Later, Hendrik Witbooi, chief of the Nama, led another rising against the Germans. He was killed in battle in 1905 and the Nama and Damara lost both their land and cattle. Peace came in 1906, but by then the loss of life and property had been enormous, and thousands of cattle had been wiped out. As a result of the final suppression of the rebellion, families and whole tribes disintegrated and the social structure of the indigenous people was shattered. The Nama population was halved, and only about a quarter of the Herero survived. Their lands and cattle were lost and many survivors fled, mainly to Botswana.

Small reservations were marked out for the Nama and

An artist's impression of negotiations between a German colonial official and the Herero tribesmen

Damara tribes, but the remaining Herero were confined to working on the farms owned by Whites.

At this time the Portuguese, who had settled in the area now known as Angola, started to conquer the northern Ovambo and a neighbouring tribe known as the Nkhumbi. Consequently, the Germans began to assert their power over the southern Ovambo and, in 1908, made treaties with them. This deterred the Portuguese from attempting to expand any further south.

The German involvement was, like all colonialism, principally for financial gain. The Germans concentrated their efforts on economic development, and helped European farmers to settle in the country. When, in 1908, diamonds were discovered near Lüderitz, there was a tremendous upsurge of interest in this

35

barren and neglected part of the world. The new industry and the general prosperity which accompanied it brought work opportunities to the indigenous people whose traditional way of life had been so severely damaged as a result of the fighting.

As the British controlled Walvis Bay, the Germans built a jetty at Swakopmund to provide an outlet to the sea. Swakopmund was linked by rail to Windhoek. Whilst the Germans were in power, they introduced the idea of "homelands", for certain ethnic groups in the southern and central districts. The population in some areas, particularly diamond-mining regions, was limited to the police and others employed there. But in

The Lutheran church in Windhoek, reminiscent of German architecture

Caprivi there was hardly any German influence or presence. Remote areas of Kaokoland were ignored and the Ovambo and Kavango peoples there were left to fend for themselves.

Evidence of this era of German influence is to be seen in the buildings which still stand in many towns, where visitors feel they would be looking at a German town in Europe. There are even castles, reminiscent of the Rhine area. German culture still appears in numerous aspects of life in the country.

However, events in Europe led to the end of German domination in Namibia. The First World War broke out in 1914. The British Navy captured Lüderitz Bay at the beginning of the war. German occupation of the territory ended in July 1915, when the German forces surrendered to units of the South African forces, acting on behalf of Britain. For the remainder of the war (which ended in 1918), Namibia was administered by the South African Defence Force.

Namibia after the First World War

Having been defeated in the First World War, which lasted from 1914 until 1918, Germany had to surrender all its colonies. The League of Nations, an international organization which was set up after the war with the aim of preserving world peace, was to supervise the way these colonies were governed.

A leading politician in South Africa at that time was General Jan Smuts. The British war-time prime minister, Lloyd George, had asked General Smuts to join his war cabinet, and this led to General Smuts playing an active part in deciding League of Nations policies after the war.

It was very largely Smuts who was responsible for suggesting a system of "mandates", by which the League of Nations would give control of the African and other territories of the defeated European nations to other powers.

Woodrow Wilson, the American president, insisted that this policy should be extended worldwide and so include South West Africa, which Smuts had hoped to take over for South Africa. Smuts then suggested that three different categories of mandates should be set up.

And so South West Africa became a "C"-class mandated territory on 1 January, 1921, to be administered by South Africa on behalf of the League of Nations. The "C"-class of mandate

General Jan Smuts, an important political figure in the history of southern Africa

allowed the territory to be governed almost as if it was a province of South Africa, although it was officially still subject to the supervision of the Council of the League of Nations.

After 1921, many Afrikaners from South Africa took over farms in South West Africa and the "native reserves"—reservations—which had been set up under German rule, were reduced in size. The German settlers were opposed to so many Afrikaners moving into South West Africa. One reason for this was that the German government was trying to persuade the League of Nations to return South West Africa to Germany, and it urged German settlers to support this claim. But the Afrikaner settlers wanted the territory to become part of the Union of South Africa.

International disapproval of South Africa's racial policies gradually increased. One of the conditions of South Africa being allowed to administer the territory was that an improvement in living conditions and opportunities for the Blacks should be guaranteed and that they should be treated as equals. Instead, South Africa gradually introduced the system of *apartheid*, — separate development which meant that the different races of people in the country were not allowed to mix with each other. This strengthened the racial discrimination and social injustice which had been introduced by the previous German regime. Large groups of the Black population were compulsorily moved to the northern parts of the country to make room for the Whites. Opposition to South Africa was also growing within South West Africa itself.

The League of Nations was disbanded in 1946 after the end of the Second World War. Its role was taken over by the United Nations Organization. South Africa wanted South West Africa to be officially recognized as part of its own territory. However, it failed to win United Nations approval for this and then refused to place South West Africa under United Nations supervision.

By 1948, South Africa was refusing to submit annual reports to the United Nations about South West Africa and was treating it like a province of South Africa. In 1950, the International

Court of Justice ruled that South Africa was still bound by the 1919 mandate agreement and must report to the United Nations, as the League of Nations successor. But South Africa refused to accept the Court's ruling. South West Africa was becoming increasingly important as an exporter of diamonds, copper and lead, fish and karakul wool. The territory was becoming increasingly valuable to South Africa as an earner of foreign exchange.

Many Africans opposed South African rule. In 1959, the South West African People's Organization (SWAPO) was formed, with the aim of planning and organizing attempts to obtain independence for the country under the name of Namibia. One of the founders of SWAPO was Herman Toivo ja Toivo, still one of the movement's leading figures. At this time, SWAPO's efforts were confined to peaceful negotiation. SWAPO also organized educational and medical programmes in northern Namibia, to prepare the people for independence. Other political parties also developed.

In 1960, Ethiopia and Liberia (the only Black African states which had been members of the League of Nations) brought a suit in the International Court of Justice to test South Africa's right to rule South West Africa. In July 1966, the Court decided, by one vote, that Ethiopia and Liberia had no right to bring the case. Meanwhile, South Africa's racial policies continued with the setting up of Bantustans—to which people were compulsorily moved, so that they lived in different regions according to their ethnic group.

SWAPO considered that further attempts to negotiate would be useless and so, in 1966, they began an armed struggle. It is estimated that about two thousand Black Africans were sent for military training, mainly in Communist countries.

Largely as a result of these developments, South Africa spent about fifteen times more on defence in 1966 than it had done fifteen years earlier. Many young South Africans spent their period of compulsory military service in Namibia, fighting SWAPO forces.

In 1966, the United Nations General Assembly voted to cancel South Africa's control over South West Africa by formally revoking the mandate originally set up by the League of Nations. The following year, a United Nations Namibia Advisory Council was formed, to lead the country until elections could be held by the people of Namibia. However, South Africa would not allow the Advisory Council members to enter the country. In 1968, the United Nations General Assembly adopted a resolution to rename the territory Namibia.

In 1969, the South West Africa Affairs Act was passed by the South African parliament. This act authorized South Africa to take control of revenue, commerce and industry, labour, mining and health in South West Africa. The territory thus came to hold the status of a fifth province of the Republic of South Africa. And South African security laws were extended to apply in South West Africa.

In June 1971, the International Court of Justice ruled that South Africa's presence in the territory was illegal. At the end of

1971, a meeting was held by those political parties in South West Africa which favoured the immediate withdrawal of South Africa and wanted a separate Namibian state to be set up immediately. They founded an Advisory Council for South West Africa. It included two Whites, two Coloureds and two representatives from Ovamboland, Kavango and East Caprivi. In addition, there was a single representative from each of the Tswana, Herero, Bushman, Rehoboth Baster, Damara and Nama peoples.

In 1972, SWAPO began the armed struggle in earnest. There were many clashes between South African forces and SWAPO "guerillas" or "freedom fighters", as they were variously called. These were mainly in the northern part of Namibia. The laying of land-mines was a prominent feature of these activities and many innocent lives were lost, as well as military installations being hit.

The seat of Namibian government in Windhoek

In 1973, the United Nations recognized SWAPO as the legal representative of the people of Namibia.

Since 1974, South Africa has declared itself willing to find a political solution to the Namibian question. Demands by Namibian and other African nationalist groups, for the independence of the territory, led South Africa to set up the SWA Constitutional Convention. The first session of the convention was held in Windhoek in September 1975, at the so-called Turnhalle Conference, where it was intended that Namibians who were reputedly friendly towards South Africa would prepare for independence. SWAPO did not take part.

The convention declared that Namibia should be fully independent by the end of 1978. In June 1977 a draft constitution was published, providing for an interim govern-ment until independence. A General Administrator was appointed by South Africa to lead Namibia towards a long-term political solution.

Previously, in 1976, the Security Council of the United Nations had demanded that an election be held under the supervision of United Nations representatives, so that the people of Namibia could choose their own government. In 1976 and 1977, five Western countries introduced conferences at the United Nations to negotiate Namibia's future. They were West Germany, France, Canada, the USA and Great Britain, popularly referred to as "The Big Five".

In 1978, South Africa accepted the recommendations of these five countries to hold an election supervised by the United

Nations, but agreement could not be reached on the conditions under which it could be arranged. A so-called "preparatory election", backed by South Africa, followed later in 1978. But this was boycotted by SWAPO and other nationalist parties.

The present Transitional Government of National Unity (TGNU) was inaugurated in June 1985. The National Assembly and Cabinet of TGNU have full legislative authority over Namibia, except for matters concerning foreign affairs and defence, which are still in the hands of South Africa. Legislation passed by the National Assembly will have to be formally signed by the Administrator-General, who will represent South Africa in the Territory, whilst the South African State President officially retains the right to amend or veto.

Talks are still continuing between Namibia, South Africa, the United Nations and the Western powers. The so-called Frontline African states (Angola, Mozambique, Zimbabwe, Zambia and Botswana) also give help to Namibia in a variety of ways, such as military assistance and financial backing, as well as support in international debates on the future of Namibia.

Meanwhile, steps have been taken to ensure that when Namibia does gain its independence, it will have a fully effective administration.

Farming and Fishing

About one-tenth of the money which Namibia earns from its products comes from farming, and farming provides employment for more than half the country's workforce. In normal times, when the country was not unsettled by internal conflicts, farming provided about one quarter of the total exports. In large parts of the country, especially in areas almost exclusively inhabited by Black Africans, it is still the only economic activity.

Although mining is of greater importance to the economy in terms of the amount of money which it brings in, it is farming that has the greatest influence. It offers employment, and the profits from it are kept within Namibia. Farming is also important in regional development.

There is a very marked difference between modern farming, by White farmers, and the more traditional methods. About five thousand White farmers with over fifty thousand farm-workers produce about four-fifths of Namibia's farm products. This is usually on very large farms of 4,000 to 8,000 hectares (1,600 to 3,200 acres). More traditional methods of farming, employing roughly twice as many people, supply the remaining one-fifth.

The restrictions imposed by the climate mean that farming in Namibia is largely centred on livestock. In the north, it is mainly cattle farming and, with the Afrikander breed as a basis, excellent beef cattle crosses are obtained with foreign strains such as Charolais, Simmentaler, Brown Swiss and Pinzgauer. Namibia has something like three thousand cattle ranches and nearly two million head of cattle. About one quarter of the cattle and carcasses are exported to South Africa.

However, almost half the cattle in the country are tended traditionally and left to wander freely in search of grazing. These cattle contribute only about two per cent of the country's meat production. One reason for this is that, traditionally, cattle are regarded as a status symbol and as a sign of wealth. They are usually only slaughtered for special occasions, or sold when extra money is needed. In less-developed areas, the hide of cattle is treated locally and used to make clothing and household items.

Another reason is that most of Kaokoland, Ovambo and Kavango territories, Caprivi and the traditional Bushman areas,

A flock of karakul sheep grazing in the arid grasslands

and even half of the regions inhabited by Herero and Damara people, are in the areas most often affected by cattle diseases such as foot-and-mouth, anthrax and tuberculosis. The transportation of both live cattle and carcasses is either forbidden or very strictly controlled there. But these diseases are far less common in the south of the country.

The southern part of Namibia is especially well-suited to karakul sheep farming. The world demand for karakul pelts has made this an important farming activity in Namibia. Karakul sheep were introduced into the region after the First World War. They came originally from Iran (once known as Persia). Today, karakul pelts provide a thriving industry, and are considered to be valuable export product. They are used for making carpets as well as fashionable clothes. The pelts are taken from newborn lambs—the tight, black curly wool is popularly

Goats in a makeshift enclosure

known as Persian Lamb. Karakul pelts are produced under the trade-name Swakara in the more arid southern regions of the territory. Almost all the pelts produced are marketed overseas, with Germany being the principal customer. Annual production can be as many as five thousand pelts. The karakul sheep also produces good meat.

Dairy farming does not form a large part of the country's agriculture. The income gained from dairy produce is small. There is an adequate supply of milk for local needs and only about ten per cent of the milk consumed is imported. The situation is, however, very different in the case of other dairy products—less than twenty per cent of butter and cheese is produced locally.

There is growing interest in the possibility of rearing eland— the largest of the African antelopes—on ranches for its meat and hide. Because of the excellent quality of its flesh and skin, the eland has suffered from over-hunting. However, it can be easily tamed and attempts are being made to domesticate it. The results are, so far, encouraging; there seems to be no reason why stock-rearers should not succeed in establishing profitable herds.

There is considerable potential for cattle and small stock-farming in areas which, as yet, make only a limited contribution to the production of meat. The two main problems to be overcome are the need to concentrate on quality rather than on quantity, and the need to avoid over-grazing. The development of veterinary services is also recognized as being of great importance in a country where cattle-ranching forms the backbone of all farming.

As the rainfall is generally too low to enable crops to be grown in much of the country, crop-growing plays a comparatively minor part in Namibia's economy. Apart from the boundary rivers in the extreme north and south of the country, Namibia's rivers are dry, sandy channels for most of the year. However, in some areas of Ovamboland, along the banks of the Okavango River in the north, and in the Caprivi district, where there is abundant water, the land can be cultivated successfully.

In a very few areas, crops can be grown with irrigation by using water from dams. One example is the Hardap Dam. This large area of water, about twenty-five square kilometres (ten square miles), in the middle of an extremely arid region, also provides an attraction for tourists. It is a man-made lake on the upper reaches of the Fish River, about 250 kilometres (156 miles) south of Windhoek.

Crop-growing is largely confined to the northern regions where groundnuts, millet, sorghum and sunflowers are grown. Sunflowers are cultivated for their seeds, which are used to provide edible oil and cattle fodder. These tall plants with their large yellow flowers grow in huge fields. They are a pretty sight—all the flowers turn together to face the sun and follow it throughout the day.

In the north-east, in the Kavango and Caprivi areas, some efforts have been made to develop land cultivation. Together

Pounding millet, one of Namibia's staple crops. The people move around in a circle, singing as they work

with some mixed farming (growing crops and raising livestock on the same farm), this type of agriculture is becoming more established. It provides jobs and training in new agricultural methods, as well as food. Modern methods are gradually being spread throughout the country by means of on-the-job training.

The staple food of the Ovambo people is a type of pearl barley called *mahangu*. It is very nutritious but, so far, only enough for home consumption is being produced.

Experimental farms and agricultural colleges are being introduced. A mill is already in operation in Caprivi, for the refining of basic products such as millet, sorghum and small grain. This is an important, much-needed project.

Fruit and vegetables are mainly imported into Namibia from South Africa, along with some grain and grain products, of which millet, sorghum and wheat are the most important.

Forestry is also important to Namibia's economy. The most valuable trees are teak, red syringa and a type of mopane. These are very hard woods which grow extremely slowly, so over-exploitation must be carefully avoided. The so-called Rhodesian teak tree takes almost three hundred years to attain a diameter of fifty centimetres (twenty inches) at chest height, and another variety of teak may take more than four hundred years to grow to those proportions.

Experimental stations have been set up to determine the suitability of various indigenous and imported varieties of trees. A type of eucalyptus tree promises to be especially successful.

Between 1950 and 1970, the fishing industry played an important role in what was then called South West Africa. Pilchards and anchovies were processed, mainly at Walvis Bay, and formed the basis of the industry. Canned fish, fish-meal and oil were exported to many countries. The crayfish industry was established at Lüderitz. Tonnes of frozen tails and canned crayfish, also called "rock-lobsters", were exported annually.

Until 1974, the fishing industry made a large contribution to the nation's prosperity. Since then, however, catches have declined alarmingly. The industry has been reduced to only very few fish-processing factories, which work only part-time. This is because the area has been over-fished and stocks have dwindled.

The waters off the coast of Namibia previously provided one of the richest fishing regions in the world. The original source of the plankton-rich water is far distant, in the Antarctic Ocean. It is driven northwards, rises to the surface off the African landmass and forms the Benguella Current along the shores of Namibia. It is teeming with small forms of marine life, capable of supporting great numbers of fish and creating a food chain for larger fish, sea animals and sea birds. In particular, there were shoals of pilchards and anchovies, maasbanker and mackerel.

Many creatures were already thriving on the numerous fish before the fishermen appeared. Gannets, cormorants and other sea birds had good feeding-grounds here, as did the penguins. Large colonies of Cape fur seals congregated along the coast and on the offshore islands.

As long ago as the end of the eighteenth century, English and American ships were hunting whales and seals, not imagining that they were constituting a threat to the very existence of these creatures, then to be found so plentifully. In recent years, conservationists have endeavoured to curb the slaughter of whales and seals but trade in sealskins still adds to the economy of Namibia.

Another attraction to this coast was guano—the droppings of sea birds, which lay in deep deposits. Its value as a fertilizer was not appreciated until, in the first half of the nineteenth century, shipments reached Europe from South America. This started a rush to the Namibian coast. The guano was rapidly removed for

53

Unloading the fish at Walvis Bay

use as fertilizer, and soon the traditional breeding-grounds were all but cleared of this valuable material.

Man-made platforms were erected as a substitute and were fairly successful in attracting the birds. But, as the numbers of fish declined, fewer birds congregated and the guano deposits proved disappointing.

Although the fishing industry is only a shadow of its former self, it could still come second only to the diamond industry as a source of revenue from exports. It is claimed that extension of the territorial waters would solve many of Namibia's problems, by preventing over-exploitation of this potentially rich natural resource. However, it is really greed, and failure to heed the ecologists' warnings against disturbing the balance of nature, that have brought about the drastic decline.

Flora and Fauna

Varying with the rainfall, the vegetation in Namibia changes from fairly dense bush and savannah with a few rather stunted mopane trees in the far north, to scattered thorn trees in the central region, and desert-type scrub in the south and west.

The Namib Desert is generally barren, but in certain places hardy, drought-resistant plants are found, among them the unique *Welwitschia mirabilis*.

The welwitschia is a most remarkable plant, or tree, and it is unique to this part of the world. There is hardly any vegetation within thirty kilometres (about twenty miles) of the coast. To the east of the great sand-dunes there is an area of black, gravel plateau. It is here that the strangest of plants is to be found. In particular, the largest known stand of welwitschias is in the Namib-Naukluft Park, at a site known as Welwitschia Flats.

The plant was first discovered growing in the gravel plains of the hot desert of Namib on 3 September, 1859, by a botanist named Friedrich Welwitsch. He considered it to be a most remarkable, almost incredible, living thing. Even to this day, its secrets have not really been fathomed or fully understood.

The plant was given the full name *Welwitschia mirabilis*—with the Latin word for "marvellous" added to the name of the discoverer. It is sometimes referred to as *Welwitschia bainesii*,

55

after the well-known artist Thomas Baines, who used to accompany Dr David Livingstone on his travels in this part of Africa, making scientific sketches as well as painting.

The welwitschia is, in reality, a dwarf tree, and is a distant relative of the pine. It has become stunted by the harsh environment. It is related both to the cone-bearing tree and to flowering plants. It sprawls over the gravel with what appear to be several tentacle-like, tattered leaves, produced from a thick, woody, bulbous central growth which somewhat resembles a massive turnip, roughly one metre (three feet) above the surface and three metres (ten feet) under ground. But it puts down a taproot, which may be as long as twenty metres (sixty-five feet).

In fact, there are only two leaves, each of which attains a length of about two metres (six to seven feet), but as the tips age and wither, scorched by the sun and torn by the desert winds, they become shredded into a tangled mass.

The plants are amongst the longest-living in the world. One large specimen has been scientifically estimated to be two thousand years old or more. They average about six hundred to seven hundred years. The plant is apparently sustained, in its centuries-long life, by drops of condensed water from the fog which covers the region during most mornings of the year. The welwitschia is sometimes referred to as the "Living Fossil". It is believed that some were living at the time of Christ.

There are different theories about how the welwitschia absorbs this moisture. It is not clear whether the tough, dark-green leaves absorb it directly or whether the moisture drips from the leaves into the ground, to be taken up by the root system.

There is, however, agreement that this peculiar plant provides food for many animals and small creatures, and also a protective home for some of them.

The crown of the stem is flattened and saucer-shaped, looking rather like an inverted elephant's foot. The male and female flowers are on separate plants. The female plant produces up to a hundred cone-like flowers in a season. The male plant produces an abundance of pollen which is blown about by the dry autumn winds. The cones are often quite brightly coloured; the male cones are salmon-pink and the female ones are greenish-yellow, banded with reddish-brown.

It takes twenty years before the welwitschia seeds for the first time. The plant produces many seeds, but most perish. The seeds provide food for the small herbivores, whilst the leaves are gnawed by the larger mammals which live in this extremely arid region, such as zebra, sprinbok and oryx. The remaining seeds are carried by the predominantly northerly wind to a location where a small number of them may eventually receive sufficient moisture to enable them to germinate.

Because of its climate and topography, Namibia has some of the most unusual plants in the world. Many of them, including the welwitschia, have been declared protected species. About eighty per cent of Namibia's protected plants occur in the southern part of the country.

In addition to the welwitschia, there are the weird-looking

A *Welwitschia mirabilis*—a strange plant, found only in southern Africa. It can live for hundreds of years

"elephant's trunks" or "halfmen" (*Pachypodium namaquanum*). These strange-looking plants appear almost human from a distance. They grow either in clusters or singly, against the mountainside. By all appearances, they seem to be marching over the hills. The heads, of green, crinkled leaves, are slightly bent. The spiny stems, which are rarely branched, are over two metres (about 7 feet) tall and are invariably turned northwards. For ten or eleven months of the year, and in times of drought, the plants withdraw into a state of suspended animation, waiting to come to life again. Shortly after it has rained, however, green velvety leaves appear, followed by a red-lipped, yellow flower.

There are also the diverse and relatively unresearched lichen fields of the Namib—some of the richest in the world. Small areas in the vicinity of Cape Cross have been set aside as nature reserves.

In the Namib Desert region there is little vegetation, except for succulents and the !Nara—a gourd-like plant which trails over the ground and produces fleshy fruit like melons. Some 3,500 species of plants are found in Namibia. About one-tenth of them are water-conservers or succulents.

The coastal belt of sand-dunes has its species of mesembryanthemum and many other hardy little plants. The colours of the mesembryanthemum are varied, but all very bright. Their seeds are able to remain inactive for long periods, in some cases up to twenty years. There are no real seasons in these areas of dunes, and the seeds of many plants only burst into life when there is a small, but sufficient, amount of water. They flower, creating an incredible blaze of colour in the desert, only to fade rapidly, spreading their seeds to the winds. These seeds, in turn, lie dormant until conditions make it possible for them to germinate and keep the species alive.

The geranium, or pelargonium, occurs in a narrow strip extending for about one hundred kilometres (sixty-two miles) north and south of Lüderitz Bay.

Another highly-regarded plant, cultivated in many parts of the world, is the amaryllis lily. There are several species growing wild in Namibia, and they are fairly widely distributed, from Caprivi down to areas of winter rainfall, in the south. They tend to occur in large clusters and their white to light- or dark-pink lily-like flowers present a magnificent display.

Similarly, orchids grow wild in the north-east of the country, in Kavango and Caprivi. One is a tree-growing species, living in the forks of large trees. Many of the species are threatened by advancing human activities.

To those knowledgeable in the lore of the veld, this apparent wilderness is a surprisingly rich source of food. Even the thorned plants produce tasty fruit. Tsamma melons are the principal suppliers of water in the arid areas. The !Nara melon, its fruit tasting like a cucumber, has edible seeds which are exported to several countries. (They are believed to act as a love-potion.)

Further inland and in the south the large aloes grow. The aloe is exclusive to Africa and there are three hundred and fifty different species. The ancestors of the modern aloe seem to have had an adaptable character which enabled them to colonize desert, mountain, grassland and beach. The aloe has adapted superbly to harsh and arid environments. The tough, normally spiked, leaves have an unpalatable juice; the brilliant flowers attract pollenating insects and the seeds are designed for wind dispersal.

There are twenty-five species of aloe in Namibia. One of the most well known is the *kokerboom (Aloe dichotoma)*, known popularly as the "quiver tree". This name comes from the fact that Bushmen use the fibrous core to make a pincushion-like quiver for their arrows. A whole forest of these trees grows near Keetmanshoop, where they form a tourist attraction.

There are many dwarf trees in Namibia, especially acacias.

The *kokerboom,* known popularly as the "quiver tree"

There are many different kinds of acacia tree. One is known as the water acacia (*Acacia nebrowni*), and is considered to be an indication of an underground water supply. Its thorns do not deter the giraffe, kudu, steenbok and springbok from eating the flowers and leaves, whilst elephants strip the branches, bark and leaves.

Another acacia (*Acacia nilotica*) produces green pods which have an aromatic scent. The rhinoceros likes to feed on its branches.

The *Acacia tortilis* is known popularly as the "umbrella-thorn", because of its shape. It reaches to about fifteen metres (about fifty feet) in favourable conditions, and has a spreading,

61

flattened crown. Its Latin name comes from the characteristically contorted pods, which are twisted into a tight spiral. These pods are highly nutritious, being rich in protein, and are eaten by giraffe and many antelope.

All these acacias are at their best in the spring-time. Even before the rains come, they anticipate the wet season and are covered with white and yellow blossoms, filling the air with their strong perfume.

To the north of the country, the number of thorn trees increases. Most of these are acacia, but other varieties include kaffirboom, witgat, bush willow and wild olive.

Further north still, the grasses become more abundant, the "bush" vegetation and the acacia scrub grows thicker, and the variety of thorn trees increases. The density of the trees increases with the appearance of the palm-tree belt and, to the

Acacia trees

A baobab tree

west, the baobab tree. This pattern is not, however, uniform. The areas of the east and west of the palm-tree belt in southern Ovamboland are, for example, sparsely wooded.

In southern Africa, north of the Tropic of Capricorn, the baobab is the undisputed monarch of all trees and plants. Wherever it grows, it dominates the surroundings not only because of its huge bulk, but also because of the weird appearance of its oddly-shaped branches. They look like the roots of an upside-down tree.

The baobab is a very friendly giant. It has no thorns and every part of the tree is useful. The spongy wood can be pulped to make rope or paper. The leaves can be boiled and eaten as a vegetable. The pollen of its flowers yields an excellent glue. The seeds are pleasant to suck, slightly acid and refreshing; and they can be ground into particles to make a drink in much the same way as coffee. The fruit and the pod contain tartaric acid; because of this, the baobab is sometimes called the "cream of tartar tree".

An average, mature baobab, with a diameter as great as seven metres (about twenty-four feet) will have taken about six hundred years to reach that size. Some will live for as long as a thousand years.

The palm and the baobab are found close to the well-wooded northern forest region, which stretches from the Kakaoveld across Ovamboland in the west to the greater part of the Kavango and Caprivi Strip areas in the east. It is here that most of the indigenous timber trees of the territory are found — Rhodesian teak, mahogany, mopane, marula, manketti and kiaat, among others.

The mopane is wide-spread. It is the dominant species of tree in the savannah plains. About eighty per cent of the trees in the Etosha National Park are mopane. It is remarkably well adapted to arid conditions. The leaves, which characteristically resemble butterfly wings, are arranged in pairs of large leaflets which, during the heat of the day, close up against each other to expose less of their surface to the sun. The crushed leaves smell of turpentine, due to their high resin content. The wood can burn well, even when green; since it is such a hard wood, the fire lasts a long time.

In the rainy season, caterpillars known as "mopane worms" hatch and feed on the leaves. These worms have a high protein

64

content and form an important part of the diet of many Africans, who consider them to be a delicacy when dried (in which form they can be stored) or roasted.

The marula tree produces a plum-like fruit. It may be used for making jelly or juices. It is also used to make an alcoholic drink. Bull elephants have been recorded as getting drunk and reeling about, after eating the fallen, fermented fruit of the marula.

Any vegetation which survives in the difficult conditions which exist in much of Namibia is, understandably, tough and stubborn. The Bushmen, in fact, have a legend. They say that one of the gods, when gardening in paradise, found a number of trees which he thought were ugly. He pulled them out and they pricked him with their thorns. In a rage, he threw them over the wall of paradise. They crashed to earth in southern Africa, many of them with their roots uppermost and their branches buried in the ground.

Some of the trees died; others, such as the *Moringa ovalifolia,* simply continued to grow, upside-down. The baobab tree is another tree which is sometimes called an "upside-down tree".

About thirty kilometres (twenty miles) west of Okaukuejo in Etosha National Park, there is a weird forest of moringa trees. It has the name Sprokieswoud, meaning "wood of the ghosts", (or "wood of the fairies"). The area is held in considerable awe by the Bushmen. The trees are easily pushed over by elephants for their mosture-holding, pulpy fibre.

In the west of the country, towards the dry steppe of the Kaokoveld, the trees and the bushes thin out and the grass

A Kori bustard, one of the many species of birds to be found in northern Namibia

spreads more abundantly, whilst the mopane trees and bushes diminish in size. This range of vegetation sustains an astonishing variety of animal, reptile, bird and insect life.

In the north are elephants, rhinoceroses, lions, leopards, cheetahs and giraffes; also in that region and elsewhere are sprinbok, oryx (gemsbok), eland, zebra (both plains and mountain species), wildebeest (gnu), kudu and jackals, together with many others, large and small. The variety of bird-life, too, is extensive. They range from large birds, such as the ostrich, the Kori bustard, the secretary bird with feathers that look like old-fashioned quill pens behind its ear and the magnificent martial eagle, through to small, beautifully-coloured sunbirds. Among

66

the water-birds are flamingos and pelicans; and along the coast are penguins and vast numbers of cormorants.

Of particular interest are the creatures which have evolved to enable them to live in the desert dunes—the little shovel-nosed lizard, the translucent Palmato gecko, the sidewinder snake, the golden mole and the "fog-basking" beetle. The latter are small beetles which stand quite still and raise themselves so as to catch droplets of water in the wind. This moisture collects together on their bodies and is finally drunk.

All these small creatures use the sand as protection from predators and from the fierce heat of the sun, or even as a source of food. Spiders, scorpions, crickets, flies, wasps, reptiles and moles all find sustenance and protection in the dunes which seem so unfriendly to the eyes of human beings.

Some scorpions are able to survive the oven-like heat because a thin layer of wax makes their surface impervious, and as a result hardly any moisture is lost by evaporation. There are rodents which are able, in some way not yet fully understood, to manufacture water in their own bodies from the apparently dry material which they consume. Some creatures are able to absorb moisture from the air, whereas others survive by feeding on those that do so.

The small, social weaver bird has an ingenious way of providing shade and thus conserving moisture. Together with hundreds of its kind, it builds a sunshade, thus forming a roof over what must be the world's most remarkable birds nests. Beneath the roof, each pair builds a nest of grasses and straw. It is the male who weaves the nest out of grass and straw, whilst the female supervises and criticizes. The young chicks and eggs are safe from most predators, though the large colonies of birds attract tree-snakes and the honey-badger.

One large animal which cannot burrow into the sand, but yet survives the apparently impossible heat of the dunes, is the oryx, also known as the gemsbok. This stately animal is the emblem of Namibia. It can survive for months on end in the most extreme desert conditions. It does so by means of a network of very find blood vessels in its nostrils, which has the effect of cooling the blood to a sufficiently low temperature and thus preventing brain damage.

Some small creatures reduce the absorption of heat into their

An example of a weaver birds' nest, with its unique roof overhead, thus providing shade and conserving moisture

bodies through contact with the scorching ground by balancing on only two or three of their legs at a time. The strange sidewinding progress of a Namibian adder snake also limits the amount of contact it has with the ground.

Small rodents, like the gerbil, bury themselves deep in the relatively cooler sand; and the golden mole rarely appears, except at night. It burrows beneath the surface, almost perpetually hunting for insects.

Some birds have specially adapted bills in which they carry water to their fledglings, often over very considerable distances. Others are even able to do this in their feathers.

About 100,000 square kilometres (approximately 40,000 square miles) of the country has been set aside as wildlife sancturaries, where not only game animals but also reptiles, birds and insects are protected in their natural environments. In addition, outside these areas hunting is strictly controlled.

One of the most renowned of the game reserves is the Etosha National Park, which was founded in 1907. It covers an area in excess of 22,000 square kilometres (nearly 10,000 square miles). It is one of the largest game parks in the world and attracts many visitors.

The heart of the Park is the extensive Etosha Pan. This half-dead lake is haunted by mirages and dust-devils (swirling spirals of sand). The brackish water is greatly enjoyed by game animals.

The word *Etosha* means "big, white place". Geologists believe it to have been an even more vast inland lake, millions of years ago.

This open plain is a photographer's paradise because Etosha is rich in bird life. Over 325 species have been recorded. They include the crimson-breasted shrike, which was the emblem of South West Africa. It is sometimes called "the German flag", because that used to be red, white and black—like the bird. Another attractive, colourful bird found here, is the lilac-breasted roller.

One of the animals which is not readily associated with this African land of deserts is the seal. But they are to be found in great numbers, along the coast. There is a breeding colony at Cape Cross, 115 kilometres (about 70 miles) north of Swakopmund. These are Cape fur seals (commonly known

Zebra in Etosha National Park

A seal colony at Cape Cross on Namibia's Atlantic coast

as "eared seals", to distinguish them from true seals which have no external ears). The seals migrate over great distances and their numbers fluctuate, but the Cape Cross colony is estimated at between eighty thousand and one hundred thousand individuals.

The natural phenomena and the varied flora and fauna of Namibia combine to offer an exciting panorama.

Industry in Namibia

Mining, agriculture and fisheries have long been the three main supports of the economy of Namibia. However, in more recent times the years of drought and the diminishing resources of fish have increased the importance of mining. The main mining activities nowadays are in diamonds and uranium, although the first European prospectors in the country in the late eighteenth century, found gold. The first mining activity was for copper in the middle of the nineteenth century.

One of the largest uranium-mines in the world is at Rössing, which is in the Namib Desert, sixty-five kilometres (about forty miles) north-east of the coastal resort of Swakopmund. It began its operations in 1974, after eight years of preparations.

The ore at Rössing is unique—it is the largest known deposit of uranium occurring in granite. In most other countries, uranium is found in sedimentary formations; that is, in finer particles of rocks that have been broken down by water action and left behind to accumulate through the ages.

The uranium oxide which is produced at the mine is exported to various industrial countries, to be used as a fuel for the generation of electricity. The Rössing mine is one of the world's major suppliers and it is estimated that about fifteen per cent of the world's known sources of uranium are in Namibia.

72

The mining is open-cast, with a pit which is surrounded by steps in terraces, each about fifteen metres (fifty feet) high. The pits thus take on the appearance of a vast sports stadium.

After being blasted loose, the rock is loaded onto vast 150-tonne trucks and is taken away to be crushed. The amount moved is the equivalent of a 100-truck goods train every twenty minutes, non-stop, night and day, every day of the year.

After the crushing comes grinding, and then the several chemical processes which require a quantity of water. Water is essential, but also a rare commodity in this region of Namibia. It is pumped from the sand of the river deltas to reservoirs in Swakopmund, where it is used to supply the needs of both that town and the mine at Rössing.

Many of the operations in the mining industry are highly

Workers checking samples at the Rössing mine

Part of Aramdis, a suburb of Swakopmund, where many of the less skilled workers from the Rössing mine live

skilled, but there is also a need for unskilled and semi-skilled workers. Many of the people in this work force come from rural backgrounds, and have had to completely change their way of life in order to adapt to the requirements of modern industry. Many Namibians have not previously had opportunity for education and are therefore illiterate or semi-illiterate. There is a strong programme of education available in the mining community, and both the employees and their children take advantage of it.

The housing, medical, educational and recreational facilities which are provided are often far better than many of the workers have been used to in the past. This reflects some of Namibia's hopes for the future. It has been said that the town of

74

Aramdis, some twelve kilometres (seven miles) from the mine, where many of the less skilled workers live, is a microcosm (a small-scale version) of what Namibia should become in the future, where people of widely different ethnic groups live side by side, in harmony.

The diamond-mining industry of the country is older than its uranium counterpart but even these rich deposits were not discovered before 1928. The first recorded discovery of a diamond was in April 1908, when one was picked up by a railway worker who was walking along checking the track, near Kolmanskop. He had previously worked in the South African diamond-mine at Kimberley, and had been advised by the German overseer to keep an eye open for promising stones. The stone was confirmed as being a quarter-carat diamond. (A "carat" is a measure of the weight of a diamond. One carat equals one-fifth of a gram.)

That first region was just south of Lüderitz and the area was worked out by the early 1930s. Many grand buildings were erected in Lüderitz at the height of its success and some were designed in the style of German castles. At the time, it was the richest source of gem diamonds in the world. Then the supplies were exhausted, and now only "ghost" mining settlements remain. The deserted buildings, half buried in moving sand-dunes, are now only a wry tourist attraction.

The later discoveries were around the delta of the Orange River (named after the House of Orange—the Dutch royal family) and mining is now based at the coastal resort of Oranjemund (Mouth of the Orange).

Although these two deposits are believed by geologists to have been separated by about seventy million years, they both owe their origins to the same source. They were washed down from the highlands far inland, from so-called "pipes" (which are of volcanic origin), hundreds of millions of years ago. They followed a network of rivers which combined into the then mighty Orange River. Nowadays, this river is often reduced to a trickle in periods of drought. From the mouth of the river they were swept along the coast by the action of strong prevailing south-west winds on the sea. This resulted in a long stretch of deposits along the coast north of the river-mouth, and a shorter one south of it.

The abandoned diamond-mining town of Kolmanskop, taken over by the drifting desert sands

Over millions of years, pounding waves ground and polished these gems, which were subsequently buried under innumerable tonnes of sand.

Since the discoveries, and the early rush to explore the region, the area has been heavily guarded, with the German name of Sperrgebiet (restricted region). It is remote and inhospitable by nature and, in addition, entry is strictly controlled.

This coastal strip, stretching about one hundred kilometres (sixty miles) inland is now the site of one of the most exciting and unusual diamond-mining undertakings in the world. In the last three or four decades the annual yield has quadrupled, to become two million carats a year. The quality is extremely good, with about ninety per cent being gem diamonds, as opposed to so-called industrial diamonds.

There are half a dozen areas along a one hundred-kilometre (sixty mile) stretch of coast where the desert has been piled up in terraces. Here the sand has to be cleared away in the search for hidden riches, buried in crevices in the deep-lying rock, often at a depth of up to fifteen metres (fifty feet).

Massive earth-moving equipment is used non-stop, to clear about sixty million tonnes of sand each year. It is estimated that every five years the weight of waste removed is a thousand million times more than the weight of diamonds recovered. After all the sophisticated earth-removing equipment has been used, it is finally left to the hand-sweepers to discover the hidden diamonds.

As people are aware that supplies will eventually run out,

Earth-moving equipment clears the sand to expose the diamond-bearing rock at the Oranjemund mine

there are repeated attempts to increase and improve the methods of recovery. For the last twenty years there has been so-called "beach-mining". This involves driving the sea back and holding it behind huge walls of sand. Then the scraping and searching begins at a level of about twenty metres (some sixty-five feet) below the nearby, pounding ocean. Of course, these walls cannot remain intact for long, and storms and seepage are a constant threat. There is a frantic race against time, with the expensive machinery and human lives very much at risk from impending flooding. There is no time for the more careful hand-sweeping.

A long and careful process of screening, crushing, milling and scrubbing follows the excavation, right down to final hand-sorting; all the time with strict security precautions.

Present known sources in Namibia are the world's richest known gem diamond deposits. They promise a continued substantial income for Namibia's economy for several more years. They currently form about forty per cent of the export trade. Meanwhile, a widespread campaign of mineral prospecting goes on, in an attempt to safeguard the future of mining.

The country is already well-known for its diamonds and uranium. What is, perhaps, no so well known is that a number of other minerals are also mined in quantity. They include copper, lead, zinc, manganese and tin. The most important of these is copper. The main source is at Otjikoto, a veritable hill of copper ores, near Tsumeb. It was first mined centuries ago by the Bergdama tribesmen or, rather, by their womenfolk, as the women and children were the labourers.

Manufacturing enterprises in Namibia are concentrated in Windhoek. These range from bakeries, breweries, chocolate factories and meat-processing plants, to printing works, factories producing construction materials, and engineering plants.

Only a few enterprises are established in the traditional areas. Typical Namibian industries are the production of kudu leather shoes (shoes made from the hide of the kudu are made in Swakopmund and known as Swakopmunders), marble from the quarries of Karibib, and wood-carvings and furniture from Kavango.

There are several factors which make it difficult for industry to expand in Namibia. The low population density means that there is only a small home-market for products. And there are relatively few raw materials for processing and refining; for example, coal and iron, which are both needed for large-scale industrial development, are in short supply. An intensive training programme is required to make us of the available labour force. Namibia still has to rely heavily on foreign entrepreneurs, expertise and skilled labour.

In addition, the terrain makes it very difficult to build connecting roads and railways throughout much of the country. This, in turn, makes it both difficult and extremely costly to develop the facilities (such as schools, hospitals and clinics) and water and power supplies that Namibia needs.

Opportunities for Tourism

In many countries of the world, tourism is a very important "industry", which plays a large part in the economy. However, because external and internal factors can easily and rapidly reduce the number of visitors, it is necessary to guard against becoming too dependent on tourism as a source of income.

Given more settled and peaceful political conditions and improved access for foreign visitors, Namibia has tremendous potential for tourism.

Windhoek, the capital, is situated 1,650 metres (over 5,000 feet) above sea level in the central region of Namibia. It has many reminders of the German, English and Dutch cultures, as well as a mixture of the many indigenous African cultures. It is like almost any prosperous town in southern Africa.

Windhoek is a good base for many short excursions, as well as being the starting-point for tours by road and air to every accessible part of the country.

Only twenty-four kilometres (fifteen miles) from the capital is Daan Viljoen Game Park, which contains something like two hundred species of animals. As there no dangerous predators, visitors may roam the hills and valleys on foot.

About seventy kilometres (forty-five miles) north of Windhoek is Gross Barmen, a hot springs resort with mineral-rich curative waters. The resort stands on the site of a mission established for the Herero in 1844.

To the west of Windhoek is the Spitzkoppe (known as the "Matterhorn of Namibia"). This is a group of volcanic mountain peaks rising from the arid Namib plain to a height of 1,829 metres (nearly 6,000 feet). Many rock paintings and stone implements have been found amongst the precipitous peaks of weathered granite.

In the northern region, which is served by good roads from Windhoek and Swakopmund, is the town of Kalkeld. Near by is a place named Otjihaenamaparero, where there are tracks of a dinosaur that walked there over a patch of soft clay (now hardened to sandstone) between 150 and 185 million years ago.

A view of modern Windhoek, Namibia's capital city

A fossilized tree trunk in the Petrified Forest in Damaraland

The footprints are protected and have been declared a national monument.

In the middle of mopane woodland is Khorixas, the capital of Damaraland. Near by is the Petrified Forest, consisting of a number of fossilized tree trunks, some up to thirty metres (one hundred feet) in length, which lie scattered over the open veld. They are estimated to be 200 million years old, and evidence suggests that they were swept to that location by a gigantic flood. Near the Petrified Forest is Twyfelfontein, the site of thousands of Bushman rock paintings.

To the south is the eerie landscape of a ridge of hills known as the Burnt Mountain. The region is practically without vegetation and is a panorama of desolation. But the rocks have shades of red and purple which glow like fire, especially in the

83

rays of the setting sun. In other parts there are huge mounts of cinder-like stones and even ash. Not far away, another tourist attraction is a geological curiosity of perpendicular slabs of basalt, given the name of Organ Pipes.

A site which is visited by many tourists is near Grootfontein. This is the Hoba Meteorite, the largest known metal meteorite in the world. It weighs approximately 54,000 kilogrammes (more than fifty tonnes), and four-fifths of its mass is made up of iron. It was first discovered in the 1920s, but it is not known when it fell to earth.

Further along the road towards Etosha is Tsumeb, a mining area with an amazingly rich body of ore. Altogether, nearly two hundred different minerals have been extracted, ten of which occur nowhere else in the world.

By far the most important tourist attraction of the northern region—and possibly the best known internationally, in the whole of Namibia—is the Etosha Game Park, where huge herds of animals range, as free as in the days before civilization came to southern Africa. It is undoubtedly one of the world's greatest and most important game parks.

The southern region of the country also has many places of interest to tourists.

About 250 kilometres (150 miles) south of Windhoek, is Hardap Dam, which is thirty-two kilometres (twenty miles) in length. It is the largest in Namibia. The area surrounding the dam is a nature reserve, abounding in game. The lake contains many varieties of fish which are good for sport and for eating.

Some distance south of Hardap Dam, two striking geological formations dominate the landscape. One is Makurob. Stark and solitary, it resembles a huge, gnarled finger, pointing to the sky. The Nama name for this pinnacle of stone means "Finger of God". The other landmark is the Brukkaros, an extinct volcano with a diameter of about two kilometres (one and a quarter miles), which looms darkly over the bare, sun-scorched landscape.

The main highway southwards through the country passes through the town of Keetmanshoop. This is Namibia's fourth largest town and it lies five hundred kilometres (approximately three hundred miles) from the capital. It is a neat, busy little town and it is also the centre of the important karakul sheep district.

One of the great natural wonders of Africa is a gigantic ravine, the Fish River Canyon; the second longest in the world. In places it is about 550 metres (nearly 1,800 feet) deep.

The Fish River is the longest river in Namibia, but its flow is now a mere trickle compared with the surging floods of past ages. There is now a hiking trail along the bed of the canyon, but hikers are subject to strict controls.

Amongst the desolate, rock-strewn wastes of the Lower Fish River is a welcome oasis for the hot, dusty traveller. It is the Ai-Ais Hot Springs, where a modern spa has been established. The springs which bubble up from the river-bed are rich in fluoride,

The Fish River Canyon, the second longest ravine in the world

sulphate and chloride. Many invalids, especially those suffering from rheumatism and nervous disorders, claim to find relief in these waters. The name *Ai-Ais* means "scalding hot" in the Nama language.

In the Namib region is the Namib-Naukluft Park. As well as being the country's largest nature conservation area, it is one of the most unusual wildlife reserves in the world. A popular attraction is the Sossusvlei area, which is a large dried-up clay pan, surrounded by remarkably high sand-dunes.

On the coast is Lüderitz, once a bustling port, built around a fine, natural harbour. Now, Lüderitz is only a shadow of its former self; yet it is still very attractive to tourists. Bartholomeu Diaz, the Portuguese explorer, reached the bay there in 1456 and planted a cross, naming the place Angra Pequena. Today, a replica of the cross has been set up on a high rock, known as Diaz Point.

Near by is the ghost town of Kolmanskop, the abandoned mining settlement, half-buried in sand. Offshore, lie the guano islands.

Swakopmund is a lively, charming town which was the country's only harbour during the German colonial period. It is Namibia's foremost coastal holiday resort and still has a great deal of German character. The remains of a solid iron pier and a lighthouse are popular places to visit.

Just outside Swakopmund stands an old steam tractor, which was imported in 1896 to carry goods across the Namib to the interior. It made a couple of journeys and then stuck fast, never to move again. It was neglected for years, but has now been restored and mounted on a pedestal.

Lüderitz harbour

Some thirty kilometres (nearly twenty miles) south of Swakopmund is Walvis Bay. A bird sanctuary outside the town attracts visitors to see the great numbers of flamingoes, pelicans and other aquatic birds congregated in the lagoon.

Between Swakopmund and Walvis Bay is Bird Island, a huge wooden platform built in the sea for the purpose of obtaining guano deposits from sea birds.

Along the coast is Cape Cross, where Diego Cão (who was the first European to set foot so far south in the African continent) planted a cross five hundred years ago. Near by is the Cape Cross Seal Reserve.

Covering more than fifteen thousand square kilometres (about six thousand square miles) of sand-dunes, gravel plains and a desolate, fog-bound, treacherous coastline, is the Skeleton Coast. The northern section of the Skeleton Coast Park has been

Flamingoes at Walvis Bay

A wreck on the aptly named Skeleton Coast

left as a complete wilderness area, and the only access to it for tourists is by way of exclusive fly-in safaris.

The space and sunlight, plants and people, sand-dunes and ocean breakers, birds and animals, are all elements which combine with many others to provide a marvellous tourist attraction—described as "Africa's Gem".

Problems and Prospects

Education, health care and communications in Namibia are basically well established. Telephones connect all but the most isolated places in the country, and daily radio and television programmes are broadcast. But the sophistication is concentrated in the urban areas, mainly dominated by Whites and largely controlled by them. Although the South African government has given the territory a measure of internal stability and has been responsible for some economic and social benefits, the non-White population has had only a disproportionate share of these benefits.

There are over sixty hospitals in Namibia, providing an average of about eight beds per thousand inhabitants. There are also 130 clinics. Specialist treatment can be obtained in Windhoek, which has one of the most modern hospitals in Africa, and also in Oshakati and Rundu, in the remote Ovambo and Kavango districts.

There is a good network of over 4,300 kilometres (about 2,700 miles) of tarred roads, connecting the main population centres. Even the secondary roads, over ten times the length of the tarred roads, are regularly graded and well maintained. Unique to the country are the "salt" roads of the coast, the foundations of which are actually gypsum, obtained from the desert. Rail transport is limited and used largely for goods. There are 2,340 kilometres (about 1,500 miles) of railways. Aircraft are used for transportation to more remote areas.

Twelve major storage dams supply the country with water. These twelve dams alone can hold eight times more water than all the minor dams, boreholes and rivers in the country combined. The water is distributed through nearly three thousand kilometres (about two thousand miles) of pipelines.

In the past, there has been a serious lack of educational

Weighing a young Namibian child at a rural health clinic

opportunities for the majority of the population. Compulsory schooling for non-Whites was only introduced in 1976. In the mid-1970s, seventy per cent of the indigenous population were unable to read and write. Now, eighty per cent of six to eighteen-year olds attend school. As far as possible, primary school children are taught in their own language, whether this be Afrikaans, English or one of the African languages.

In 1980, a higher education institution was set up in Windhoek. The Academy is a combination of a university, a *technikon* (which concentrates on the applied sciences) and a college for vocational training. The aim of the Academy is to create equal educational opportunities for all the inhabitants of Namibia. The number of students has increased from only twenty-six in 1980 to around four thousand. The situation whereby twenty times more money per person was spent on the education of Whites than on non-Whites is changing, although the pace of change is still too slow to satisfy many.

Christian missions have been successful in Namibia and there are many churches in the country. The churches have been active in supporting the independence movement.

Meanwhile, the struggle for complete independence for Namibia continues and is increasingly supported, in principle at least, by mounting world public opinion. This issue is clearly linked with the question of racial discrimination in South Africa.

Several factors stand in the way of Namibia gaining full independence. The politically dominant White population does not wish to give up the prosperity to be found in the country.

The opposition to South African rule by the non-White population is not united and there are many internal disputes between different groups. Those efforts which have been made to prepare for a hand over of power to independent control are viewed with suspicion by many people and are regarded as being half-hearted.

Such acts of violence as have occurred have been isolated and sporadic. The infiltration of armed African fighters from the north has not yet created a real threat to the government nor a serious challenge to its security forces.

It remains to be seen for how long the future of Namibia will be bound up with that of a White-dominated Republic of South Africa.

Index

94